Club
You ca
follow
Newca
Portsm
Blackbu
Sunderland, PSV, Arsenal, Bolton,
Middlesbrough, Manchester City,
Birmingham, Wigan, Chelsea,
Derby, Everton, Aston Villa,
Reading & Tottenham.

MY FOOTBALL YEAR

MANCHESTER UNITED

BY REGINALD DRINKWATER

A GENUINELY UNIQUE AND PERSONAL
ROUND-UP OF MY TEAM'S SEASON

Choose the front image

Your club here
In this 2007/8 season we have a wide
selection of top clubs on offer for you to
choose from (see list above).

You're the author
This is your chance to own a book with
your name as author on the front, edited
and published by you and representing
a uniquely personal view of the ups and
inevitable downs of your season.

Document your team's season...

Heartbreak in Athens – the pain is all too real for Xabi Alonso after Liverpool's agonising defeat

After every game our researchers will select the best pictures taken at the ground to give you a choice of images for your book.

You pick the one that depicts a telling moment from the game, or that sums up how you felt immediately after it. You can even add an appropriate caption.

REGINALD DRINKWATER'S FOOTBALL YEAR 2007–08

Filippo Inzaghi rounds Pepe Reina to net the winner in Athens

A frustrated Benitez appeals another decision

So near yet so far – Crouch picks up his runners-up medal

A night of missed opportunities for Kuyt and Liverpool

Jermaine Pennant consoles his captain, Steven Gerrard

You can create a spread of memorable images from the month. It's simple with our drag-and-drop software, which even resizes the photos for you.

MAY

QUOTES OF THE MONTH

"At the moment my heart is in two pieces. It's the lowest moment of my career, but it's how you bounce back from set-backs that counts."
— Steven Gerrard

"I wonder if Crouch felt insulted. I would have in similar circumstances. Crouch, an England forward, left out in favour of a midfield player."
— Tony Cascarino

"Rafa got it wrong on the night. Pennant was the right choice but we should have started with two forwards and played Gerrard in the centre of midfield."
— Reginald Drinkwater

Decide which quotes from the pundits and stars you want to feature in the book and add your comments alongside the best of them.

REGINALD DRINKWATER'S FOOTBALL YEAR 2007–08

...from your perspective

Don't agree with our headline? It's simple to overwrite our words with your own, summing up your memories of the match.

Use the reports written by our professionals or write your own personal slant on the game as you saw it.

We have a team of statisticians who will capture all the key data from each match. We present these as graphic panels and you decide which to include.

FA Cup Final 19th May 2007

DROGBA'S CLASS SETTLES 'NEW WEMBLEY' FINAL

Kiss this! – Didier Drogba lights up Wembley with a moment of brilliance to seal the FA Cup for Chelsea

**MANCHESTER UTD 0
CHELSEA 1**

Didier Drogba's clinical finishing lit up a 90,000 crowd to win the first cup final at the new Wembley.

Chelsea's player of the year raced onto Frank Lampard's return pass to clip the ball past the on-rushing Edwin van der Sar and into an empty net.

It was a rare moment of genuine class as the Premiership's two exceptional teams all but cancelled each other out for most of the game. There was plenty of goal-scoring talent on both sides but the game turned into a midfield battle with neither team able to find a way through until Drogba's 116th minute goal saved us from penalties.

Stand-in centre-back Michael Essien looked the part alongside John Terry, while John-Obi Mikel and Claude Makelele prevented United's dangerous midfield from ever hitting its stride.

Lampard came closest in the first half. His running put him behind the United defence to receive a clever ball from Paulo Ferreira but van der Sar saved his cross-shot. The midfielder then connected with a 30-yard drive that flew narrowly over.

Wayne Rooney tested the Chelsea defence with some powerful running from deep in the second half without ever threatening Petr Cech. Jose Mourinho's half-time substitution of Joe Cole for Arjen Robben, caused Wes Brown some nervous moments at right back.

Both sides have played over 60 'cup finals' in reaching the Champions League semi-finals and contesting the Premiership to the end of the season, before reaching Wembley's showpiece and both tired as the game want into extra time.

Cech's only real test came when Ryan Giggs slid into the six yard box and made a poor connection with Rooney's cross in the first half of extra time. Giggs' momentum carried both Cech and the ball over the line but the ref neither gave the goal or a foul and although the decision was muddled the outcome was the correct one.

Drogba had a rare sight of goal beyond United's far post but headed wide. Then with the spectacle of penalties looming, a United attack broke down and Chelsea launched their decisive raid too late for United to come back.

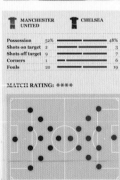

	MANCHESTER UNITED	CHELSEA
Possession	52%	48%
Shots on target	2	3
Shots off target	9	7
Corners	1	6
Fouls	20	19

MATCH RATING: ★★★★

Venue Wembley, **Kick-off** 15:00
Referee Steve Bennett, **Attendance** 89,826

CHELSEA		MAN UTD	
Cech	7	Van der Sar	7
Ferreira☐	7	Brown	6
Essien	7	Ferdinand	7
Terry	7	Vidíc ☐	8
Bridge	6	Heinze	7
Makelele ☐	7	Carrick	8
Mikel	8	Scholes☐	8
Lampard	8	Fletcher	5
Wright-Phillips	5	Giggs	7
Cole	5	Ronaldo	6
Drogba	8	Rooney	8

Subs: Robben (for J Cole 46) 7; Kalou (for Wright-Phillips 93) Y; A Cole (for Robben 108) Y. Not used: Cudicini, Diarra.

Subs: Smith (for Fletcher 92) Y; Solskjaer (for Giggs 112); O'Shea (for Carrick 112). Not used: Kuszcsak, Eora.

STAR PLAYER
Lampard – he was always in the thick of the action, had two of Chelsea's best attempts on goal and set-up the winner with his quick thinking and return pass.

REGINALD DRINKWATER'S FOOTBALL YEAR 2007–08

REGINALD DRINKWATER'S FOOTBALL YEAR 2007–08

Premiership 6th May 2007

ARSENAL 1
CHELSEA 1

José applauds spirit but it's United's title

Reduced to ten men and a goal down with the Premiership title heading to Manchester, Michael Essien launched the Blues' comeback.

It wasn't quite enough to bring the win they needed to prevent United taking their crown, but it epitomised Chelsea's grit and belief.

The game seemed lost in the 43rd minute when Khalid Boulahrouz found himself out-muscled by Julio Baptista. The Dutch defender hauled his opponent down and was correctly red. Gilberto Silva converted the resulting penalty.

Without Didier Drogba or Andriy Shevchenko, it was left to Essien to head Chelsea level and the Blues should have won it from there. Joe Cole saw his attempt disallowed, Essien blazed another chance over and Frank Lampard's long-range drive tested Jens Lehmann.

Venue Emirates Stadium, **Kick-off** 16:00
Referee Alan Wiley, **Attendance** 60,102

ARSENAL		CHELSEA	
Jens Lehmann	7	Petr Cech	6
Emmanuel Eboue	6	Paulo Ferreira	7
William Gallas	7	Khalid Boulahrouz	3
Kolo Toure	7	John Terry	7
Gael Clichy	7	Wayne Bridge	7
Vassiriki Diaby	5	John Mikel ⬚	6
Cesc Fabregas	5	Michael Essien ⬚	8
Gilberto	8	Frank Lampard	6
Denilson	6	Shaun Wright-Phillips	7
Julio Baptista		Joe Cole	7
Emmanuel Adebayor ⬚	6	Salomon Kalou	6

Subs: Hleb (for Denilson 59) 6; Hoyte (for Diaby 79). Not used: Almunia, Senderos, Djourou.

Subs: Diarra (for Mikel 74) 7; Sinclair (for Wright-Phillips 80). Not used: Cudicini, Makelele, Sahar.

STAR PLAYER
Essien – refused to believe he couldn't keep the Blues in the Championship race and almost did. His energy made up for the loss of Boulahrouz.

Michael Essien celebrates securing a point at the Emirates

Premiership 9th May 2007

CHELSEA 0
MANCHESTER UNITED 0

United game comes too late

The guard of honour gesture stuck in the throat as United only fielded a team of reserves and youngsters at Stamford Bridge.

This game was supposed to be the title decider and may have been just that if it had been played on its original date in April. A win over United then could have caused their title form to wobble. As it was, two under strength sides played out a meaningless goalless draw, with the Premiership already decided.

Both sides were saving the serious business for the cup final clash at Wembley although Scott Sinclair impressed in his full debut for the Blues. Another good prospect, Ben Sahar, came on to force a clearance on United's line as Chelsea had the best of the game.

A lacklustre game sinks to second-half handbags

Premiership 13th May 2007

CHELSEA 1
EVERTON 1

Blues level home unbeaten record

Chelsea levelled Liverpool's record of 63 home games unbeaten in the league with this final game draw against Europe-bound Everton.

Jose Mourinho fielded a strong team to secure the milestone.

The record was threatened when Salomon Kalou blasted a clear chance over the bar and James Vaughan responded for Everton by slotting a 50th minute goal. However, the unusually misfiring Didier Drogba scored his 20th goal of a great campaign, converting Shaun Wright-Phillips low cross to preserve the record.

Kalou and Ben Sahar tested Howard before the end but it was Everton who finished the game aggrieved after James McFadden followed up a powerful Lee Carsley drive to convert from Petr Cech's parry, only to see his effort controversially ruled offside.

Venue Stamford Bridge, **Kick-off** 15:00
Referee Mark Halsey, **Attendance** 41,746

CHELSEA		EVERTON	
Petr Cech	8	Tim Howard	7
Paolo Ferreira	7	Tony Hibbert	5
Khalid Boulahrouz	6	Joseph Yobo	6
John Terry	6	Alan Stubbs	6
Wayne Bridge ⬚	6	Joleon Lescott	6
Frank Lampard	5	Philip Neville	7
John Mikel	6	Leon Osman	6
Joe Cole ⬚	5	Manuel Fernandes	5
Shaun Wright-Phillips	7	Lee Carsley ⬚	6
Didier Drogba	8	Mikel Arteta	6
Salomon Kalou	7	James Vaughan	8

Subs: Sahar (for Cole 70) 6; Morais (for Mikel 74) 6; Hutchinson (for Bridge 89). Not used: Hilario, Sawyer.

Subs: Beattie (for Vaughan 72) 6; McFadden 6 (for Fernandes 77). Not used: Turner, Naysmith, Vidente.

STAR PLAYER
Cech – enhanced his reputation as the world's best keeper with a superb save from James Vaughan's acrobatic volley, which proved crucial to the result.

Chelsea's incredible home record is preserved by Drogba's equaliser

---

Determine which stats you think best tell the story of the game. You can use the line up panel to give players marks out of ten.

If you have more to say about a game you can swap out other elements to make more space for your match report.

Who was the game's star player? In this book, you can choose the man-of-the-match and also add a paragraph to give the reasons behind your decision.

How it works

Use the interactive website to edit pages and create your book.

At the back of this book is a sealed plastic wallet containing a password. It is your ticket into this one-off experience, enabling you to register at the My Football Year website:

www.myfootballyear.com

Once logged on, enter your club and open up your book.

It doesn't matter that the season's already started – your book is already filled in with all the reports, stats and pictures of every game played. You can go back to past games and start customising it straight away. As soon as you alter a man-of-the-match, change a player's performance rating, or swap in a different picture, your book is unique.

Use our journalists' reports and headlines or write your own. You can decide if you want to write more on a particular game because you were there, or criticise the manager's selection.

Your book is available at the end of the season, whenever you are ready to print. Even if you add nothing, you still get a brilliant book, capturing the quotes, action and images of your club's season. However, we hope you use all the simple web-tools and extra content we provide to make your book truly exclusive.

Full details of how to register are with the password card on page 17.

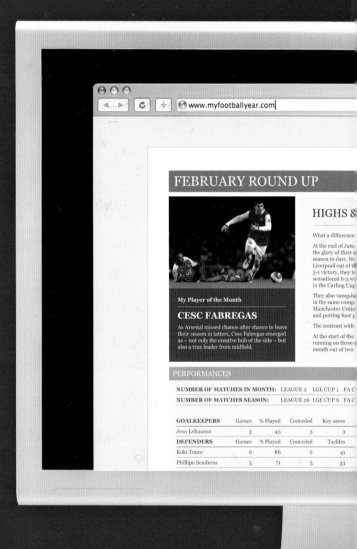

FEBRUARY ROUND UP

My Player of the Month

CESC FABREGAS

As Arsenal missed chance after chance to leave their season in tatters, Cesc Fabregas emerged as – not only the creative hub of the side – but also a true leader from midfield.

HIGHS &

What a difference

At the end of Janu the glory of their season to date. No Liverpool out of th 3-1 victory, they to sensational 6-3 wi in the Carling Cup

They also vanquis in the same comp Manchester Unite and putting four p

The contrast with

At the start of the running on three month out of two

PERFORMANCES

| NUMBER OF MATCHES IN MONTH: | LEAGUE 2 | LGE CUP 1 | FA C |
| NUMBER OF MATCHES SEASON: | LEAGUE 26 | LGE CUP 6 | FA C |

GOALKEEPERS	Games	% Played	Conceded	Key saves
Jens Lehmann	3	43	3	3
DEFENDERS	Games	% Played	Conceded	Tackles
Kolo Toure	6	86	6	41
Phillipe Senderos	5	71	5	33

www.myfootballyear.com

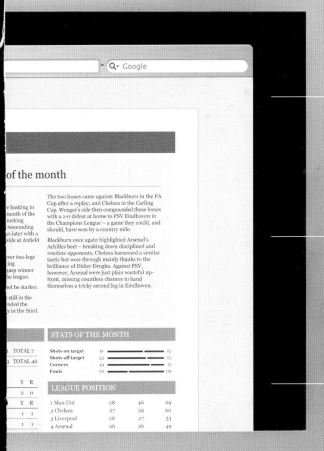

of the month

The two losses came against Blackburn in the FA Cup after a replay; and Chelsea in the Carling Cup. Wenger's side then compounded these losses with a 1-0 defeat at home to PSV Eindhoven in the Champions League – a game they could, and should, have won by a country mile.

Blackburn once again highlighted Arsenal's Achilles heel – breaking down disciplined and resolute opponents, Chelsea harnessed a similar tactic but won-through mainly thanks to the brilliance of Didier Drogba. Against PSV, however, Arsenal were just plain wasteful up-front, missing countless chances to hand themselves a tricky second leg in Eindhoven.

STATS OF THE MONTH

Shots on target	41	23
Shots off target	53	25
Corners	44	15
Fouls	60	119

LEAGUE POSITION

1 Man Utd	28	46	69
2 Chelsea	27	29	60
3 Liverpool	28	27	53
4 Arsenal	26	26	49

You have our team of writers, designers, statisticians and photographers working on your book and updating your pages on the website after every game.

Go online and you can change their words, swap their picture for a different one, switch to an alternative design or select a different stats panel.

The changes happen before your eyes and your book takes shape over the season. Click on, change, click-off; our software does all the hard work.

Write your own headlines

OUTCLASSEI

becomes...

ROBBED BY I

Every game is 90 minutes of tortured grimaces and fist-clenching exhilaration. At the last lingering blast of the whistle, you either want to dissect every misguided selection and poor substitution, or revel in each brilliant performance.

My Football Year lets you write your own reports, or change ours, to suit your view of the game. My Football Year shows you how to add your own headlines, include the pictures you choose and rate the performance of your players – and because it is web based, you can update it from anywhere in the world.

Our match reports will be short, but should you wish to write more about a game then you can. Simply click to remove a stats panels and click again to open extra space for your reports. We provide plenty of research material.

There's a simple guide on the website to help you extend your report or write a blow-by-blow account of the game's action.

AT UNITED

LIND REF!

Choose the images

A picture is worth a 1000 words –
Each month of the season features
a picture spread that captures its
unforgettable moments.

Top sports photographic agency Action Images has its photographers at every big game and their picture researchers will be working through hundreds of photographs after each game to select best shots for your book.

A look at August's pages on the website will show what we've chosen, but you can select different ones if you want.

Moving pictures around is easy 'drag and drop' so provided you can use a mouse, you'll have no problems using the pictures you want.

Select the stats

Statistics are the bare bones of a football game: a hard record of who was on the pitch; how the teams lined up; and how many corners, fouls and goals were conceded.

We'll provide you with a full range of relevant and accurate stats in a series of superb 'stats panels' allowing you to decide which set you want to include.

Picking your star players

Often a TV pundit's or newspaper's view of how your team's performed will be completely at odds with your own.

It's time to do something about it!

After every game our reporters will give each player a mark out of ten. One of the stats panels on offer is a line-up panel where the ratings will appear. If you don't agree, that's fine because you can overwrite them to give your view on each individual's performance – it's your book after all...

Another panel you can include highlights the game's star player. We will pick one for each game, but feel free to swap our choice for the player you consider to be man-of-the-match.

Whether you change our choice or not, you can write a caption explaining why the chosen player was the star on the day.

Finally, you can rate the game for the quality of football or for its entertainment value.

Capturing the highlights

We also want you to be able to flesh out your book with the highlights you'll remember: a description of a goal... a wrongly flagged 'offside'... a penalty decision that changed the course of the game.

To help you record these highlights we have designed a commentary panel. We will fill this in for each game based on what we consider to be the key moments but if you think differently, you can change them to suit your take on the game.

The bare facts

There will also be a stats panels that include:
– possession
– shots on and off target
– corners
– yellow and red cards

At the end of each month we will round up your team's progress with league position and details of their scorers. We will look to improve and expand these features through the season based on your feedback.

Prioritise matches

Some games will stick in your mind at the end of the season. It may be because you were there, you watched it with friends, or a particular incident or memory makes it a special game to you.

Those are the games we hope you will devote extra attention to in your book. Of course, it's impossible for us to know which games they will be, so you get to choose.

Each month we'll select what we think are the most important games and give them extra space. Our designs work with one, two or three game reports a page. So in a typical month with five fixtures, two of our pages, will feature two games and a third page will be wholly given over to a big match.

However, you can change this order. Perhaps you went to the first game of the month so you want to devote the full page design to that game. All you need to do is shuffle the full page report to the start of the month.

Let's get started...

By providing you with all the tools and support you need, we will help you create a book you will treasure and be able to share with friends and family at the end of the season, and for years to come.

Hopefully the last few pages have left you excited if not a little astonished – after all you are taking part in a publishing first. Now it's time to check out your club's season so far and see your book coming together.

To do this, follow these step-by-step instructions:

1. Take your password card (it's on the page opposite). First check it hasn't been tampered with. If it is broken you must e-mail us straightaway at security@myfootballyear.com
2. Log onto www.myfootballyear.com
3. Enter your password exactly as it appears on the card
4. Follow the on-screen instructions

There is a further security question and we will require your address to ensure we send your book to the right place. We will also require an e-mail address and phone details in case we need to contact you or spot a problem with your files.

Once you have successfully registered, you should change your password to something you can remember but which other people who know you would find hard to guess. If you have any concerns about security there's also form on the Feedback section of the website. Please take the security seriously as it exists to ensure you are not disappointed.

This password gives you editing privileges and the right to print your completed book. It's your responsibility to keep it secure until you hit the PRINT button next summer. Now you can click on the first month, August and see what we've included and start to move pictures, edit reports, captions and headlines. Have a good mess around. We will only file the changes if you press the Save Changes link.

You will be the author, editor and publisher of your book giving you the freedom to write whatever you want. With this, however, comes a responsibility: to act within the publishing laws; avoid libelling anyone and to refrain from breaching anyone else's copyright. There are guidelines on the website and you are unlikely to do any of these things unless you are determined to do so. A complete set of terms and conditions are available when you register so please read them carefully as you will be asked to accept them before you can send your book to be printed.

This is a completely new concept in book publishing and we are keen to get your thoughts. There is a feedback form on the website and as we go through the season we will take on board your views and use them to improve and increase the features we can offer you. So remember the elements described here and features shown are illustrative and subject to change during the season, often because we have made these improvements.

www.myfootballyear.com